teach me about

# Mealtime

Copyright © 1984 by Joy Berry
Living Skills Press, Sebastopol, CA
All rights reserved.
Printed in the United States of America

No part of this book may be reproduced by any mechanical, photographic or electronic process, or in the form of a phonographic recording, nor may it be stored in a retrieval system, transmitted, or otherwise be copied for public or private use without the written permission of the publisher.

Managing Editor: Marilyn Berry
Copy Editor: Orly Kelly
Contributing Writer: Kathleen McBride
Contributing Editors: Georgiana Burt, Radhika Miller
Design and Production: Abigail Johnston
Illustrator: Bartholomew
Composition: Curt Chelin

Grolier Enterprises Inc. offers a varied selection of both adult and children's book racks. For details on ordering please write: Grolier Enterprises Inc., Sherman Turnpike, Danbury, CT 06810 Attn: Premium Department

# teach me about Mealtime

### By JOY BERRY

*Illustrated by Bartholomew*

GROLIER ENTERPRISES CORP.

I do not want to get sick.

I eat good food.

Good food helps me stay well.

I want my body to grow.

I eat good food.

Good food helps my body grow.

Mommy and Daddy love me and do not want me to get sick. They want my body to grow. They give me good food to eat. I eat the food they give me.

Mommy and Daddy love me and want me to know about all the good food there is to eat. They ask me to taste food I have not tasted before. I taste the food they give me.

I may get sick if
I eat too much food.
I eat only when I am hungry.
I stop eating when
I have had enough.

I may get sick if I eat or drink
too many sweet things.

I do not eat too much candy.

I do not eat too many cookies.

I do not drink
too much soda pop.

Food is not a plaything.

I do not play with my food.

I do not want to make a mess when I eat.

I try not to get food on myself.

I try not to get food on the floor.

I use special things to help me eat.

A plate holds my food.

A cup holds my drink.

A spoon or fork helps me get food into my mouth.

I use these things carefully.

I do not want to burn my mouth.

I wait for my food to cool if it is too hot to eat.

I do not want to choke on my food.

I do not put too much food in my mouth at one time.

I chew my food very well before I swallow it.

I do not want to get a stomach ache.

I eat my food very slowly.

I do not want to get sick.

I want my body to grow.

I eat good food.

# helpful hints for parents about
# Mealtime

Dear Parents:
The purpose of this book is
   to motivate children to eat good food, and
   to provide children with guidelines for eating.
You can implement the purpose of this book by
   reading it to your child, and
   reading the following *Helpful Hints* and using them
   whenever applicable.

## NURSING MOTHERS

Here are some suggestions for easier mealtimes if your baby is nursing:
- Get plenty of rest, drink lots of fluids, and eat high protein food for adequate milk production.
- Use a bed rest for comfort when nursing in bed.
- Catch up on needed rest by occasionally sleeping through the night, while your partner supplements the middle-of-the-night feeding with a bottle.
- Offer water daily to the nursing baby, especially in warm weather.
- Store breast milk by freezing it in sealed, boilable pouches. Date the pouches, then freeze them up to 3 months. To use the stored milk, check the date on the pouch, then immerse it in warm water to thaw.

## FORMULA FEEDING

- Check the expiration date on formula containers before purchasing and using the formula.
- Wash and rinse the tops of formula cans before opening them.
- Follow the mixing instructions on the formula container carefully to get the maximum nutritional benefits for your baby.
- Cover and refrigerate any open can of formula. Once the can has been open, the formula must be used within 24 hours.
- When formula has been mixed and the bottles are filled, they should be kept cold until they are warmed for a feeding.
- Keep a bottle cold when you leave home by placing it in a sealable plastic bag and packing the bag with ice.
- Keep a bottle warm for up to an hour by wrapping it in a washcloth and placing it in a tennis ball can with a lid.
- Warm a cold bottle fast by placing it in a microwave oven, **uncapped,** for 30 to 60 seconds.
- Test formula warmth by shaking a few drops onto your wrist. It should be no warmer than body temperature.

- Hold your baby during feedings to enhance the bonding between you and your child.
- Create a relaxed mealtime atmosphere, free of tension, while bottle-feeding your baby.
- Do not put your child to bed with a bottle as it can cause serious dental problems.

## BURPING YOUR BABY

Here are some suggested techniques for burping your baby:
- Cover your shoulder with a diaper and lift your baby onto your shoulder. Gently pat your baby's back or rub it, using a circular motion.
- Lay a diaper or towel on your lap and place your baby on his/her stomach. Gently massage or pat your baby's back.
- Sit your baby on your lap facing away from you. Brace your baby with one hand while you pat him/her with the other.

## BOTTLE CARE

Follow these suggestions for taking care of your baby's bottles.

### Bottles and nipples

- The dishwasher works well as a sterilizer for your baby's bottles and nipples. Hang nipples from the top rack of the dishwasher inside a mesh bag.
- Sterilize nipples in the microwave oven by putting them in a glass jar of water with one tablespoon of vinegar added.
- Place clogged, gummy, or hard nipples in a pan of water with one teaspoon baking soda added. Boil the nipples for several minutes. Rinse, dry, and then store them in a covered glass jar.
- Remove a sour milk smell by filling the bottle with warm water and one teaspoon of baking soda. Shake well and soak the bottle overnight. Wash it in the morning.

- Boil bottles for ten minutes in a pan with one cup of vinegar to remove chalky residue.
- Remove fruit juice stains from bottles by filling them with warm water and one teaspoon of dishwasher detergent. Shake at 15-minute intervals until the stain has loosened, then rinse thoroughly in hot water.

## WEANING YOUR BABY TO A CUP

When you and your baby are ready for weaning, you may want to try these suggestions:
- Remove the nipple from the bottle and allow your baby to drink from the bottle.
- Put a little milk in a cup and tip it just enough to get one sip at a time.
- Introduce a plastic cup with a detachable mouthpiece at mealtime.
- Offer favorite drinks in a cup and less favorite drinks in a bottle.
- Be patient while weaning, especially during teething or illness.

## FEEDING YOUR BABY SOLIDS

The following is a list of equipment and utensils which are useful for feeding your baby:

- A highchair or seat with attached tray.
- Plastic bowl, plate, and cup with handles. Those with suction cups attached will not slide. Plates with edges work well.
- Child-size eating utensils or a sturdy plastic spoon, knife, and short-tined fork.
- A TV tray, paper plates, shaped baking pans, and cupcake tins create variety in serving meals.
- Several bibs made from fabric or soft plastic.
- A damp cloth or moistened towelettes.
- Extra spoons to replace those that drop.
- Small toys or washable hand puppets for entertainment.
-

### Safety at Mealtime
- Never leave your child unattended in a highchair.
- Provide a well-balanced highchair to keep your child from rocking or tipping over.
- Be sure the footrest on the highchair is well attached to give your child proper support.
- Apply nonslip appliques on the seat of your child's highchair to prevent him/her from slipping out of the chair.
- Place your child's highchair out of the way of foot traffic and away from doors and windows.

### Feeding procedures
Here are some suggestions for feeding your baby:
- Introduce new foods at the beginning of a meal when your child is hungry.
- Offer one new food at a time in order to identify any possible allergic reaction.
- Serve small pieces of new foods in sizes small enough to chew.
- Use a blender or food processor to prepare some of the family's meal for baby.
- Let your child feed himself/herself by providing easy-to-handle finger food.

### Suggested foods
Choose from among the following foods and cut them into bite-size pieces:
- apples (steamed)
- bananas which have been coated with dry baby cereal to make them less slippery
- bagels
- bean curd
- berries
- breadsticks
- broccoli (steamed)

- cauliflower (steamed)
- carrots (steamed)
- cheese—a variety
- frozen fruit juice bars
- grapes
- graham crackers
- melon slices
- noodles (cooked)—a variety
- orange slices
- potatoes (steamed)
- raisins
- rice cakes
- toast from a variety of whole grain breads
- zucchini (steamed)

More finger food ideas:

- **gelatin blocks:**

    4 envelopes unflavored gelatin
    1½ cups cold fruit juice
    1½ cups hot fruit juice (heated to boiling)
    2 tablespoons sugar (optional)

Sprinkle gelatin over the cold juice in a medium bowl and let stand one minute. Add the hot juice and stir to dissolve gelatin. Add sugar if desired. Pour into an eight- or nine-inch square pan and chill until firm. Cut into one-inch squares.

- **vegetable dip:**

    Steam a variety of vegetables and provide yogurt, ricotta cheese, or cottage cheese as a dip.

- **high-protein drinks:**

    Add an egg, yogurt, protein powder, or all three to eight ounces of milk or fruit juice in a blender. Serve in a baby bottle or cup.

- **homemade baby food:**
  Blend steamed vegetables in a blender and freeze in ice cube trays. Store the serving-size vegetable cubes in sealed plastic bags and thaw for serving.
- **protein cones:**
  Fill an ice cream cone with tuna or egg salad, cottage cheese, or thick yogurt.

## MEALTIME CLEANUP

Here are some suggestions to make mealtime cleanup easier:
- Put a dab of baby oil on your child's face before meals.
- Tuck soft tissues or paper towels under your baby's chin before tying on the bib.
- Lay a plastic drop cloth or an old shower curtain on the floor under the highchair.
- Serve your child's meals outside in warm weather.
- Hose down and scrub messy highchairs outside.
- Cut a hole in a paper plate and poke the stick through the hole when serving juice bars.

## ATTITUDE TOWARD EATING

- Let your child's appetite determine how much food he/she eats.
- Never force, threaten, bribe, or punish your child about eating.
- Teach your child this principle: "Eat to live rather than live to eat."
- Provide the freshest, most nutritious foods possible for your child.
- Expect appetite changes in your child with illness, growth, or any changes in routine.